LOOK FOR ME IN JUNE

Finding Your Pet After Rebirth

By
Karen A. Bowen

Published in the United States of America by
Ariadne Publishers, Brookfield, WI, U.S.A © 2016,
414-444-2012.

All rights reserved.

ISBN: 0-9649343-7-X

Dedications

To my father, Osmo Kalevie Larmi Sr., whom many lonely, abandoned and abused dogs followed home. And, who taught me loving patience with the helpless ones.

And, most importantly, to that still small voice of conscience, the infallible counsel of the inner voice, that guides us all along the way.

Acknowledgments

All of the animals who have graced my life with their love, presence and blessings.

All of my clients and animals who taught me so much about the love and sacred pact we have with each other.

My beloved husband, Richard A. Bowen, who has been so patient, loving and kind throughout all of our times.

Pauline Adams for the cover photo and her support along the way.

Contents

Dedications 2

Acknowledgments 2

Preface 5

Introduction 6

PART ONE – It All Began with Christmas 8

    How Quickly Things Change 14

    Simba and Her Kittens 19

    Socializing and Finding Homes 22

    Daring Rescue from a Not Great Home 25

    Changing Times 28

    His Passing, So Much for Appearances 30

    Now What? 32

    Next Step 34

    He Is Back 35

PART TWO – Over the Years 38

    Butchie and Pudgy 40

    Learning to Care for Injuries 42

PART THREE – My Work with the Care, Death and Rebirth of Pets 46

    One Dog Ready to Make Her Transition ... 48

    Puppies from a Dying Mother 51

Finding the Right Dog to Rescue 53

Finding Your Pet After Death 55

An Alaskan Spitz Returns As 57

Preface

They stand by as silent (sometimes) sentinels offering us unconditional love, compassion and gentle affection while we undergo the major changes of our lives. They do not care if we are old or young, rich or poor, healthy or sick. They simply see us through the ever changing landscapes of our lives being the always faithful, kind and loving companion.

How do you write about the purity of love a dog or cat brings into our lives? Are there words that even describe the patience, compassion and forbearance they demonstrate?

For anyone who has ever had a beloved pet, *Look for Me in June* offers consolation that death is not the end.

Introduction

Look for me in June contains the true story of the saving grace and love of a dog so dedicated to his owner that he reincarnates three times to help her through difficult life challenges. It is one story of the love and friendship that goes beyond the portals of birth and death.

What attracts us to our pets? Why did you pick yours and not mine? Is it the body, the coloring, the breed? Or is there something more important, more sacred than outer appearance? Is it possible that our pets pick us as much as we pick them? Do we have a sacred pact with each other and a sacred responsibility to the critters who come into our lives? I believe we do. I believe in the oneness of all life.

If you look at our beautiful planet from outer space it looks like a giant beach ball, full of color, splendor and magnificence. Everything on that ball has a purpose, a connection to every other part. What seems separate is in actuality part of the one sphere we call Earth. We often feel what occurs in a so-called distant land has nothing to do with us. That radioactive waste from the Tsunami in Japan won't affect our health. That war and bloodshed in the Middle East has no impact on our lives. That destruction of habitat through drilling for oil in pristine natural areas won't come back to haunt us.

That's like thinking that cancer on one of our toes isn't affecting the health of our whole body.

And so, I believe it is with each and every one of our lives. I believe what appears to be random, separate events of individuals and beings entering and leaving our lives are actually part of a magnificent scheme. A scheme which includes a school to teach each of us some very valuable lessons. And, that these lessons test us, as well as, goad and guide us to become more fully awake to the power of choice that we have as humans. That we are actually responsible for the tone and flavor of our lives, our successes and failures. And, that we cannot ignore our rightful place as caretakers of the portion of the planet that we inhabit. Nor can we ignore or deny the important place our pets play as they teach, comfort, correct and love us.

PART ONE – It All Began with Christmas

It was Christmas time and I was at the lowest point of my life. I had lost my job, my Porsche had been repossessed, my Siamese cat had died and I was trying to stretch unemployment benefits to pay rent and utilities, as well as, feed myself and my surviving cat, "Divot."

Divot had come to me when I lived in Detroit and worked as manager at a Fortune 100 company. One day as I was playing with a three-some on a golf course we saw a large brown paper bag fly out of a moving car on the freeway. After the bag cleared the fence and landed on part of the green, a tiny white and orange kitten emerged, shook himself and walked towards me. I ran over, scooped him up and left the game. Divot would be his name.

Now, six years later after leaving my well-placed position, going through a divorce, and a total reverse of fortune, I had to borrow my mother's old Chevy to get around. It was Christmas Eve and I was driving on a busy highway in blizzard conditions when I saw a dog on the side of the road. I didn't need another mouth to feed but compassion won out. The truth is, it is impossible for me to ignore an injured, abandoned or abused animal. I stopped the car, gently encouraged him towards me and lifted his packed-with-snow body onto the front seat. He seemed to acquiesce to the idea of my help. After a few minutes I observed him intently scratching himself. Pulling back his white fur I noticed he had three or four fleas on every inch of his body. When I got him to my apartment it took four full baths and rinses before he was clean. After a short while together I realized he wouldn't bark, lick or jump up, and, he was terrified of staircases. It must have been an unfriendly place he was escaping.

Despite his past and how he must have been treated, he was an amazing gift of Joy in my life. He loved everyone and just about every animal. He and Divot became fast friends. I decided to stop trying to find him a forever home with someone else and named him Christmas.

Christmas

We became inseparable. His limit was six miles which we hiked together each day for the first two years. He was there with me as I scrounged for work. I was either over qualified or under qualified for all the managerial positions in my new location of Milwaukee, so I ended up doing some office work for small business owners in my building.

It was an up and down time. When the times were hard I would sell off some furniture and belongings to pay for food and rent.

In my daily prayers for guidance I kept hearing "continued vacation, different view." The meaning escaped me as I certainly did not consider my situation as a vacation.

Fear began to grip me when I was down to my last possessions: my clothes, a single bed, a futon on the floor as a couch, and a living room chair. Losing my apartment and being put out in the street loomed in the very near future if I could not find more work. I became overwhelmed with the idea of my pets going without food or a home.

Then in answer to my prayer I heard a clear, "Call Joanie." Joanie Yates was a friend of mine who had lived in the building but moved when she got divorced. I was too ashamed to call her and tell her about my plight. However, each time I prayed I got the same answer.

Finally, in desperation, I got the courage up to phone and explain my situation. Her response amazed me, "Call Norb. He has an apartment in your building as a mail drop. He may let you use it."

Norbert was her ex-husband whom I had met one time. I took a chance and phoned him. After reminding him of who I was and explaining my situation, he said, "Sure, you can use my apartment, it is on the top floor facing the north shore. My lease runs for another ten months and I never go into the apartment. I simply use it as a mail drop when I am on the road. When I am in town I stay with my girlfriend." Wow, I was in awe.

After explaining that I would do my best to pay him back, he declined my offer and simply said, "You be an angel for someone yourself. That will be payment enough. All the rent and utility expenses are covered by my company, the only thing I ask is that when the lease is up, you clean the apartment and return the furniture they supplied so I can get my deposit back."

Astonished I went to talk with the building manager to tell her of my good fortune and the move. She gave me a key and confirmed that a table and chairs had been supplied to the apartment.

As I opened the door to the one-bedroom penthouse apartment, I saw that it faced north with a view of Bradford Beach and the north shore communities. My studio had faced south with a view of Lake Park Lagoon, Lake Michigan and downtown Milwaukee. This was definitely a different view and I would find the new apartment was the answer to the prayer reply I received, "continued vacation, different view."

After my move to the 23rd floor of the Prospect Towers life changed dramatically. Christmas was witness to me falling in love, marrying my soulmate, Rich, and many amazing adventures. He was calm and sweet despite what must have seemed like an endless round of moving to new apartments and situations. He was patient when we had to hide him in the laundry basket to take him out to relieve himself when we lived with Rich's mother between stints in a "no pet" condo.

He reveled in being the only dog allowed and basking in the love of all the tenants when we were apartment managers for 104 units on the East Side.

Then there was the freedom of living on Lake Michigan in Door County during our sabbatical when I wrote my first book. Although that adventure was a bit tarnished by his chasing a porcupine and catching it.

He made peace with the passing of Divot, his old buddy, who died of cancer. And the addition of Precious, a skin and bones kitten whom my sister had found in a dumpster. Somehow my sister thought the kitten was mine and presented her to me as a birthday gift.

Precious

Finally, after 10 years we were able to buy a home with a yard for him to play in. The day before the move I took him and Precious, who had by this time been with us for five years, to see their new abode. Christmas' eyesight was bad and he walked very slowly surveying the new territory. Precious was her normally curious self. I was so happy that they finally had a forever, never have to move again, home.

In the middle of the night Rich woke me to tell me that Christmas was gone. My groggy response, "How could he get out?" thinking that somehow the dog had found his way out of our apartment.

"He's dead," Rich whispered.

I was stunned. "How could he die? Why would he die just before the new home?"

I walked into the living room where his body lay in front of the patio door. No release of urine, just one small drop of blood on the carpet near his mouth was all he left. "Just as graceful in death as he was in life," I thought.

Sadness gripped my heart and I began to shake and cry. Then I heard inwardly a gleeful voice, "But Mama I'm free, I'm free!"

The sound of joy in those words did not stop the pain in my heart or slow the flow of tears.

His decline was apparent. There had been no six mile hikes for quite some time. But, I never expected this.

The move to our new house was filled with sadness instead of joy. It was easier for me to take his body to the Humane Society for cremation. I just couldn't handle burying him.

We decided, "No more dogs. It is too painful when they die."

How Quickly Things Change

Just six short months later, near my birthday in August, I got an intuitive hit to look for a puppy. "No way," Rich said, "I don't want to go through that again." So I began the search by myself. I had long known that following my intuition was the only way for me to be happy and successful. And, to ignore it now, well that wasn't an option.

I found a pet store a mile from our new home and decided to walk over to check it out. Sadly, it was closed. When I told Rich what happened, he said, "I'll go with you next time."

Entering the pet store the next day, I was attracted to a Schnauzer puppy. However, when the shop owner placed him into the play pen the puppy totally ignored us, his eyes following a small child on the other side of the store.

Meanwhile, Rich was observing a white puppy with brindle ears in a crate. "What about that one?" he asked. As soon as the puppy was on the pen floor he ran to me then to Rich, back and forth, back and forth. "Well I guess you are coming home with us," I said.

Chakotay Bear

A few years earlier while reading a book by Richard Bach titled, "One," I had become aware that the same "soul" of an animal can return to its owner. For some reason, the idea had not crossed my mind even though the puppy's behavior was extraordinary. It was as if he were saying, "Okay folks, I am back. Let's go home I want to play in my yard."

It took four days to find a name for the pup. He would not respond to anything until we called him Chakotay (Cha-Koh'-tay), a name we got from the Star Trek Voyager series. We added "Bear" as a middle name later.

Unlike Christmas, Chakotay was wary of people and would bark at them then run away. He would torment "Precious" until one day when she decided to show him who was the alpha animal.

Chakotay Bear and Precious

As he jumped towards her on the couch she swiftly reached out with both paws, grabbed his head, bit him on the nose to draw blood and, bingo, that was all it took.

All the dogs in the neighborhood were also to be avoided. He seemed to be afraid of everyone and everything except us.

Then, several peculiar events made me begin to think he might be Christmas returned.

One day as I was walking him he was particularly slow, stopping, stopping and more stopping. Pulling on the leash and calling his name had no effect on him. So I began to count to ten as I had with Christmas. Yes! At the count of nine he moved on just as Christmas had. "Hmmmmm," I thought.

The deciding moments came when we went to visit a friend, Torin Lee, who had been Christmas' dog sitter. Remember, Chakotay was terrified of everyone and every dog. Surprisingly, when we got to Torin's apartment building, he ran up to her door and began jumping and barking. When she opened the door, he tried to jump into her arms. And the final, tell-tale, he was not afraid of her big yellow Lab, Eddie. In fact, he chased the lumbering dog around the grass area, nipping at his ears, getting even for previous injustices, I am sure.

Now, we were convinced. Chakotay was the re-embodiment of Christmas.

He was very loving to us and easy to train being a foodie. He learned the standard tricks: speak, lay down, roll over, sit, and up. However, when I tried to walk him farther than just around the neighborhood, he would slow down and then stop. There was no budging this puppy once he laid down. His distance limit was one mile, a far cry from Christmas's six-mile limit. He was also terrified of the crate and riding in the car.

Later, we found out he had come from a puppy mill in Green Lake, Wisconsin which easily explained his poor health and stamina, as well as, his unease with people, other animals and crates.

In January, after he had been with us five months we decided to take a long road trip to Sedona, AZ. He made it to Oklahoma Avenue, a distance of 4 miles, before heaving up the first time. The 18-hour trip was miserable. We tried everything to help him cope. Little did we know at the time that it would take years before he stopped throwing up in the car.

The next difficulty came with my having clients in the home, which was always a pleasure with Christmas. One day a mother who was reading while she waited for her child's session to be over called out to me. Chakotay's fear of people turned into barking and growling and my client was afraid to move off of her seat.

Fortunately, we had a Dutch door between the main house and our family room where I would isolate him while I worked with individuals and their pets. However, his barking then became problematic.

Soon I came to realize the only way he would warm up to people is if they fed him many, many times. So to help him socialize, I had clients and their children give him treats for doing tricks. It was a very slow, laborious process but finally paid off.

He came to love family and friends that fed him, as I would say, "42 times." He became so attached to my sister, Claudia, that he would literally pull me the half mile to her house. She always had treats for him and he had learned to put up with her yappy Shih Tzu, Gabriel.

He was happy to greet our friend, Pauline, and would jump up on the couch to sit by her. Nevertheless, if I sat on the couch as well, he would move over to where I sat and lean in to me. It was as though he was reassuring me that he loved me more.

One client, Barb L, made a special impression on Chakotay. After a "treat" session she would get down on the floor to play with him. He accepted her loving kindness and came to trust her so much that he would eagerly go to her home and spend time with her Alaskan Spitz, Jules. Barb became our vacation pet sitter extraordinaire.

Simba and Her Kittens

Chakotay's tolerance for other animals improved as he witnessed me helping 19 feral cats through the Milwaukee Feral Cat program. This rare opportunity allowed me to humanely trap stray cats so they could be vaccinated, neutered and occasionally find a forever home. Those who did not want to be domesticated were returned to the neighborhood to live out their lives on their own terms.

I had been feeding a group of released ferals when a white and gray Calico cat that I named Simba showed up. After coming daily for several weeks, on an April morning, she brought four kittens with her. A neighbor who lived a block away told me the kittens had been born one snowy day in January in the back of a convertible in a yard near her home.

It was with Simba that I learned about female cat behavior. Two of the kittens were tan tabbies, one was a multi-colored tabby and the fourth was a long haired grey kitten.

Simba began to bring them twice a day to eat on the covered patio. I wanted to gain their trust so each day as they ate I tempted them with a play mouse on a string. As the days went by the kittens became more interested and venturesome coming closer and closer to catch the mouse. However, Simba stayed aloof.

Then one morning I heard a horrible cat scream and looked out to see Simba with four male cats. The kittens were huddled in a corner of the patio. My first thought was the males were threatening to kill the kittens, and Simba was protecting her family. However, the males were there on a different mission. Simba was in heat again and the males were there to service her. One male was a yellow tabby, one a long haired grey cat, one pure black and the other a non-descript mixture. Oh, this is how she had four kittens that looked very different. They came from different fathers.

Not knowing any better, I got the water hose out and broke up the party. It was then I decided I had to trap her and the kittens fast before more kittens arrived.

The problem was, I knew I might not be able to trap them all in one day. And, even though they were eating well, and sleeping in a small tree nearby, I did not want to separate Simba from her kittens. I decided to pick the kittens off one at a time so that the remainder would stay safe with their Mom.

The first one to fall for my game was the only male, the alpha yellow Tabby. I had placed several cat carriers open on the patio so they could become accustomed to their presence. One day during our play time I threw a toy into one of the open carriers close to me to see if anyone would chase it. Yes, he did, and boom, I closed the door. He was frantic for a bit until I covered the crate with a bath towel.

That evening when I got him back from the Humane Society, I decided to put him into the sunroom in

Chakotay's large dog crate. I equipped it with four shelves for sleeping along with an area for litter and one for food and water.

It took me three days to catch the kittens as I was lucky enough to catch two at once. After they were all safe in the crate in the sunroom I was ready to trap Simba. The problem was she had not shown any interest in playing and had stayed far away from me when I put out the food. Did she want to be domesticated? Did she want a forever home?

I knew once she came back from the Feral Cat Process I would be bringing her into our home and working to socialize her.

I decided to ask Simba about her future. To make sure I was being unbiased, I invited our friend Pauline, who also understands pets, to tune in with Simba at the same time. We sat on the patio as she was eating and asked her spirit if she wanted to be domesticated. Both of us got a resounding, "No."

It was clear that she would be returned to the neighborhood and not placed up for adoption.

Only human tuna would entice Simba into the humane trap. And, after her return from the Humane Society she came each day for several weeks to eat and look in the window at her kittens. Then we didn't see her for a long time.

One day while walking the dog Rich thought he saw Simba dead on Congress St. a block away. She appeared to have been hit by a car. I had to see for myself so I walked to the corner. Fortunately, and sadly it was another cat. Simba did show up one more time, probably to let us know she was fine. And then we never saw her again. We pray she is well.

Socializing and Finding Homes

I had actually never socialized feral kittens before. However, I figured the more I could handle them and get others to do the same, the better. So, I began a routine with each one after they returned from the Humane Society. Twice a day at feeding time I would coax one of the kittens out of the crate with yummy food. However, before they were allowed to eat each kitten got combed, belly rubbed and cuddled. Then on to the food outside the crate and the next kitten. After eating they had the run of the ten foot by sixteen-foot sunroom as we played.

When they were safe in the crate I would let Precious and Chakotay into the room each day to see if they would adapt to having a playmate or two. Precious never did. It was always serious hissing and her hitting the crate with her paws. The kittens would fly to the farthest part of the crate and huddle in terror.

Chakotay on the other hand was at ease. A bunch of kittens in his crate was fine with him as long as he did not have to go into the crate with them.

The multi-colored alpha female was very sweet and playful. I named her Angel because she acted as a mother to the others letting them eat first. She was the largest kitten, loved attention and actually laid in my lap while the others played.

Tiger and Angel

The tabby alpha male I named Tiger. He loved to play but found it difficult for me to hold him. It took a lot of playing, coaxing and patience before he was relaxed and trusting.

I named the long hair grey kitten, Delilah because of her long fur and her sister in size but not demeanor, the little yellow tabby, I named, Pee Wee.

Pee Wee got her name because even before I trapped her she would climb up on the lannon stone ledge around our house, walk to where I was sitting in my office and meow until I brought out the food. She never shut up and still performs the same ritual daily, only now it is inside our new home.

When it was time I placed an ad, "Free kittens to great homes." First a young woman from Kenosha called about my ad. When she arrived to view the kittens, she was immediately attracted to Angel and wanted to take her home. However, my policy had several conditions. After speaking with him or her on the phone the interested person had to come to our home to see the kittens and for me to see them and question them. Then I took the kitten to the prospective home to make sure it would be a great place.

The day for giving up Angel was very difficult. I had become attached to her and she to me. After driving the forty odd miles to Kenosha, the woman's apartment turned out to be bright and clean. And she was obviously very sincere about wanting Angel, having prepared everything for her before we arrived. After walking around, the apartment just to make sure, I reached into the crate to get Angel. She came easily but did not want to leave my side. She kept looking up at me and meowing. I spoke words of comfort to her as I stroked her back and belly and told the young woman that if Angel did not adapt within a week, I wanted her back. She agreed.

I cried as I closed the crate door and left the apartment. Was I doing the right thing? Maybe Precious would accept Angel and I should keep her.

In a few weeks I received photos. Angel had taken over as queen of the apartment. I was at peace.

Placing Tiger was easy. The young woman interested in him had a cat in need of a playmate. Her apartment was only a mile from our home and although it was not as tidy as I prefer, I could see that she really wanted the kitten. We set up a crate and play area for Tiger to be gently introduced to her cat, with the agreement again, that if it didn't work out, I got Tiger back.

She called in a few weeks. Everything was fine.

Daring Rescue from a Not Great Home

I wanted the last two kittens to be adopted together. Pee Wee and Delilah were not only litter mates, but now with their siblings gone, they were clinging to each other in every way.

Many people called, some of them with really weird stories of why they needed two kittens. One woman called several times with a different story each time. She even gave me her neighbor's number as a reference. When I called the neighbor, he said the woman was nuts and was cruel to cats. Great reference.

Just a few people came to see the kittens but nothing felt right and I remained determined that they would only go to a great home.

Then a man called needing a playmate for his cat that lost his brother. The man and his girlfriend stopped by and despite the "beater" car seemed to be fine. They were willing to adopt both girls so I arranged to deliver them the next day.

Their apartment was on the second floor of an Oak Creek apartment building, just a 25-minute drive. After walking in, I left the girls in the crate on the floor so their cat could smell them and until I was comfortable with the set up. Their cat was a large male who was very friendly. They explained that his brother had gotten out somehow and was poisoned by antifreeze, thus the need for another cat.

I noticed he had not been altered and questioned them about that. After talking for 20 or 30 minutes, I felt comfortable enough to leave the girls there. I had brought food, toys, litter and was willing to leave the crate so the girls would have a familiar place to go during the introductory period.

The couple assured me that everything would be fine and they would take time getting the three acquainted. However, that evening at bedtime I began to feel really bad about the girls. Something seemed wrong. I called the couple and they again assured me that everything was fine.

The next morning the feeling of dread was still present. I called again but got no answer. Something was wrong.

I asked Rich to accompany me back to Oak Creek in case I needed his help getting the girls back. I did not know why, but the feeling of dread persisted.

As we drove I hatched a story I would tell the couple as an excuse to get the kittens back.

We did not buzz the outside door as it was cracked open. So we simply and quietly made our way upstairs. When I knocked on the apartment door, the young woman answered. She was surprised to see us and again said the kittens were fine. As I rushed past her I told her that I was really worried about the girls especially since their sister (a lie) would not stop howling for them.

As I repeated my story over and over, I hurriedly got their crate and asked her to bring them to me. She called out, "Kitty, kitty," but no one replied and she could not find them. She explained that her boyfriend would be very upset if we took the kittens back, as he really wanted to keep them. Fortunately, he was not around.

I called out their names and heard Pee Wee screaming, but couldn't find her. Frantically looking everywhere, I lifted up the table cloth and found Delilah cowering and pinned against the back of a dining room chair with their big male cat threatening her nearby. I scooped her up, put her in the crate, closed the door and handed it to Rich.

Again, I called to Pee Wee, this time I followed the scream and found her trapped between the side of the kitchen counter and the refrigerator, a space barely big enough for her to squeeze into. It was clear she was trying to get away from the big bruiser male as well. She had jammed herself in head first and as I pulled at her hind quarters she screamed in horror. Finally, once I got her free and cuddled her, she allowed me to place her in the crate.

While the woman objected, we headed for the door, kittens in tow. I told the woman she was welcome to keep the food, toys and litter as we ran down the stairs.

Once outside and in the car, the feeling of dread disappeared. My intuition had been right. The girls were in danger but now they were safe.

Delilah and Pee Wee

Changing Times

Chakotay was four years old when Pee Wee and Delilah came to stay for good. I am sure at times he felt outnumbered by the three cats, all female. Nonetheless he kept his cool.

Precious on the other hand did not fare as well. The three felines tolerated each other for a while. But as the kittens grew they began to get even for all of her bullying. Perhaps their experience with the big bruiser male had sparked some courage or "Sisu" in them.

Just like Christmas, Chakotay would be with us through many adventures. He would survive being attacked by a "friendly" German Shepherd who broke free of his owner in the park and clamped onto Chakotay's hind leg leaving a puncture wound. Unfortunately, at the time we did not realize the event would cause him to develop Cushing's disease from the stress.

Little did we realize that all would change in five short years.

He was with us through the wonderful moments of our love and the toxic moments leading up to our break-up and divorce. At all times he remained magnanimous, loving us equally.

After the divorce, we lived together a short time in our common home until I moved to Michigan taking Pee Wee and Delilah with me as they were so attached to me. Rich, having stayed in the home, kept Precious who was suffering from cancer and Chakotay who by this time could no longer walk.

The day I had to leave them was immensely painful even knowing that Rich would do everything to keep them comfortable and happy.

After a few months, my situation in Michigan changed and I returned moving into a home in Wauwatosa. In December Rich asked if I would come to the house to care for Precious and Chakotay while he went on a vacation to Florida. When I visited the home I was devastated by their condition.

Rich was doing everything he could but they were both declining so rapidly and I could not bear to see the dog splayed out on the floor, his back legs paralyzed and he unable to move.

I asked, "Are you sure it is fair to let them continue in their condition?"

With tears in his eyes he replied, "I don't want to cut their lives short by one second."

We prayed and both knew it was time to let them both go.

His Passing, So Much for Appearances

As he lay on the floor, his frail body limp and surrendered, his glorious hair now replaced with wisps of cottony fuzz on his neck, head and hind quarters, he looked abused and neglected. Patches of dark pigmentation and scores of calcified lumps covered his thin, wrinkled skin. His appearance denied the truth—he was a cherished and beloved dog.

Kneeling close together on the floor of the family visiting room at Animal Emergency, we cradled Chakotay in our arms.

On the couch nearby, with her own stifled tears of sadness sat our dear friend, Pauline, holding Precious who would be next. Pauline had answered our desperate plea to drive the car so we could focus all our attention on these last few minutes with them.

Chakotay Bear was, after all, the first dog she had come to love and, therefore, her dog too. Rivers of tears poured down our cheeks as we wept and cried out loud at this sad farewell to our beloved Lhas-Kimo. The veterinarian had already inserted the picc line for the injection. Chakotay had given out only a tiny yelp. Our bodies trembling with grief, we hugged him, blessed him and reminded him how much we loved and cherished his presence in our lives.

Not wanting to cause him one more moment of discomfort, I murmured a sobbing, "Okay." With her kind and gentle touch, the young vet inserted the needle and he was gone. More hugs, more tears and then wrapped in a blanket he was taken to be cremated. It was December 19th, he had been with us a short 11 years, 4 months and 6 days.

Still weeping, Rich and I embraced to comfort one another. The pain in my chest was so intense, I thought my heart would stop. On and on the sadness grew. Then, like a sweet, new breeze, I inwardly heard a quiet voice whisper, "I'll be back—look for me in June."

Then it was Precious' turn.

For some reason, I was more surrendered with Precious. Her life as the playful "attack cat" who would go for walks in the forest following the dog had morphed into one of a recluse. It had been hard to get close to her. Perhaps her early life of starvation and survival in the dumpster had left her with so much mistrust that she couldn't be trusted. Then with the cancer and the other cats ganging up on her in revenge for how she treated them as kittens, I knew she was ready for a new life. Her passing was kind and swift.

As we prepared to go home, my mind returned to Chakotay. Over and over the thoughts rolled through my mind, "Did he know how much I loved him? Did he know the grief I bore for his passing? Did he understand the anguish of making the decision to put him down? Did he want to die? Was it his time? Why did he wait until this day to pass? Why did he withstand so much difficulty? Could I have done something different? Should I have taken him with me to Michigan?"

I don't remember if I shared the message with my companions that day. It was impossible to think about the future with so much pain in the present. But I did remember suggesting to Chakotay a few days earlier that he could come back to me if he wanted to, once he passed on.

Later that evening I wrote the whispered message in my journal, "I'll be back—look for me in June."

Now What?

Rich and I went back to our separate lives after Precious' and Chakotay's passing. However, we still attended the same church and had the same friends so we often spent time together and I realized that despite the divorce and all the pain it had caused, we could be friends.
In January the owner of the house I was renting decided to put it up for sale. As I began looking for another place Rich suggested I move back to the house we owned together until I found another suitable place. He had kept my area separate and it was available for me to use, but I was happy living by myself.

Then in February after suffering with daily headaches as well as a persistent throat irritation and harsh cough, I found out the house I was living in had Radon levels high above allowable limits. This Radon poisoning was not only a risk to me but also to my clients some of whom were vulnerable children.

The owner of the house was in Asia on business and difficult to reach. Rich suggested I move back in with him until the problem was sorted out. My clients would only be exposed to an hour or so each week whereas I was exposed 24/7.

So after many discussions of how we would live in the same house but have separate lives I moved enough into the home so I could sleep there and conduct business out of the rented home in Wauwatosa. I brought Peewee and Delilah back with me not wanting them to be exposed to the toxic Radon atmosphere.

On April 17th, I decided to do some work in the backyard of our shared home and as I was digging I saw Chakotay run towards me. The vision was so real a wave of sadness hit my heart and I began to weep. I so missed my dog.

When he was a puppy and a healthy adult, I had to travel a lot for my work. Back then, he would be so excited to see me when I returned that he would piddle all over the ground. So Rich would bring him outside to greet me. I loved that dog.

Next Step

Soon I began to feel stuck between the old and the old. I asked myself, "Why am I living in two houses? One that is not mine and one I only have a part in?

I was feeling cramped sleeping in one room at my old home and sharing the kitchen. Our relationship had become frayed and we were starting to get testy towards one another. At my rented home there was a lot of room but I was being subjected to toxic gases and it was up for sale.

I began to look more earnestly for another home and office.

In early May I still had not found a home that would accept my two cats and have room for an office. When I got back to the house after work one day Rich had dinner prepared for me. As I was placing the cats' food on the floor I saw a dog waiting right next to them. It was an ephemeral vision but recognizable just the same. Then, during dinner Rich said, "I think God is playing with us, because we own the house together and we have been given a chance to get along. We have the chance to create a really happy life where we really enjoy ourselves." I knew he was right.

I began to pray for clarity about my situation and at one point the answer came, "You must finish with Rich." I did not know what that meant so I continued to inwardly seek the answer over the next week. One day as I was meditating I saw a picture of Hiawatha and Minnehaha who were well known as spiritual partners. I asked inwardly, "Are Rich and I spiritual partners?" and I heard a clear, "Yes."

He Is Back

On Memorial Day, I dreamt of a puppy in a cage peeing on something like cotton. Shortly after that our friend, Pauline, came for a visit. As she walked in the door she said, "Every time I pull up to this house I see a white dog in the yard."

I knew she meant a vision of a white dog and not one in physical form. I replied, "He must be back in a body because I saw a vision of him run to me in the back yard. Then I saw him on the floor one day when I was feeding the cats, and I dreamt of him and now you tell me you keep seeing him in the yard."

I told Rich I thought Chakotay was back in a body. But, he was still grieving his loss, so I began to look for him by myself. I went to the Humane Society several times, but my dog was not there. I looked on line at Golden Doodles because I was convinced he would come back as a big dog, but nothing felt right.

Then on June 24th Rich and I prayed about whether or not we should go together to look for him and both got a "yes." We went to the Humane Society to look at a puppy named Zsa. But, no, it was not our dog.

The next day as I prayed I heard inwardly, "He is a Teddy Bear." I went online for information and found two places in Milwaukee that had Teddy Bears. We went to the closest one first.

Before getting out of the car we prayed to be shown if our dog was there and which one it was. After walking through the front door, I proceeded to walk straight ahead and look in each crate. As I peered into the fourth crate I heard Rich call out, "He's over here. You don't have to look any further. He barked three times at me when we walked in the door."

Not believing Rich, I took my time and walked around the perimeter of the room. Once I got to the crate where he was standing, I immediately knew which of the two puppies was ours. The attendant put him in the play pen. As he ran around and played with the other puppies waves of joy swept over me. Running fast, jumping over the other puppies, he was so happy with his new puppy body. I called to him and reached down to pick him up. He jumped up and was immediately at ease in my arms.

We were unsure about his sister still in the crate. Should we take her as well? "No," came the answer. There was another home for her.

The Universe, God, had conspired with us to find our dog again. All we had to do was ask for guidance and trust our intuition. What Joy, what Joy, what Joy, we both felt.

After completing all the paperwork and instructions, Rich carried him into the car. First stop — to be reunited with the one who was there on his last day in the previous body, Aunt Pauline. We called her from the car to make sure she was home. When we arrived she met us in the driveway. She sat down on the pavement and as soon as we put him down he ran to her waiting arms. He remembered!

The three of us sat on the driveway in amazement at the miracle of this reunion. The puppy was at home on Pauline's lap. Unlike his incarnation as Chakotay where you had to feed him several times before he warmed up to you, now it was remembrance and love at first glance.

We took him home and he immediately chased Delilah and Peewee. "Here I am again," he seemed to be saying, "This time in a swift and playful body." And, they remembering him, accepted his playful energy to a point, then rushed off to hide.

After this brief flurry of activity, he did something that changed my belief system forever. He was not yet three months old and too small to jump very high. So I gently lifted his body up on the couch and we played for a while. I was going to assist him down but before I could, instead of jumping or sliding down from the edge he took a flying leap as if he was doing a swan dive. He was showing me just how happy he was to be back, to be in a new body, to be healthy again.

I will never worry about euthanizing an animal ever again. He has proven to me every day that life is sweet and to be enjoyed. Our pets drop their bodies and pick up new ones like we discard clothes that are old and of no use.

Our bodies may be like annual flowers and appear only once, but our souls are perennial.

I have always known my pets were great blessings in my life. Throughout the years, cats and dogs have been my companions through life's toughest challenges.
However, it was not until I made the conscious choice of asking Chakotay to come back that I saw the power of their love, compassion and our sacred pact in my life.

Chakotay II

PART TWO – Over the Years
My early life with animals

My first memory of a pet was as a toddler with the family dog, Rover, a big red dog, probably a Labrador Retriever mix. Besides table scraps, the only food our dogs got were dog biscuits. I remember sitting on the floor in front of the kitchen cupboard containing the biscuits with Rover at my side. I would break a biscuit in two and say, "One for you and one for me." I remember to this day the gritty taste of the dog biscuits. I guess I figured if he could eat people food, I could eat dog food.

Dogs frequently followed my Father as he walked the two miles home from work. He loved dogs and would spend a lot of time combing and brushing them. However, along with his example of love and compassion I learned a lot about the cruelty of humans.

Between my first memory of Rover and my entry into junior high school there were four more dogs that passed through our home. Taking a dog for a walk was foreign to my family. It was customary to let the dogs out to do their "business," as my Mother called it. However, we lived at a busy intersection and several of our dogs were killed by cars.

I remember pictures of me at age four or five with Fritzie, a large, long-haired black and white dog that looked like a Border Collie. And Trixie, a short-haired white and black spotted dog that looked like a Chihuahua when I was six or seven.

For some reason, either I was too young, or my parents shielded me from the trauma, I do not remember how Rover, Fritzie and Trixie died.

The next dog that came via Dad was a white Alaskan Spitz we called Spitzie. My Mom was against owning a female because of their proclivity to get pregnant. My parents never had any of our dogs "fixed" as they would say. So, of course, Spitzie was allowed to run free. One evening she came home and laid on the porch with blood running from her mouth. When Dad and I rushed her to the vet we found out that someone had fed her ground glass mixed into ground meat.

That was the first overt act of cruelty I experienced and nothing my Father said could help me understand why someone would do such a horrible thing to an innocent, sweet animal. Father and I cried together.

Then, my older brother found a little short-haired white, tan and black dog that we called Patches. Unfortunately, she died soon afterwards from an enlarged heart. What caused it, we never found out.

Butchie and Pudgy

When I began junior high school a tan, short-haired, tall, stocky, mongrel type dog came home with Dad. Butchie was a happy dog and a lot of fun. He would run so fast when he came into the house that he would drag all of the small area rugs with him as he skidded down the hallway into the kitchen. However, along with his happy fun, Butchie had one bad habit, chasing cars. My two older brothers had enlisted in the Air Force so I was now responsible for pet care and I did everything I could to break this tendency, but nothing changed him.

One day as I walked the two miles home from our church downtown I found a little reddish-tan puppy in the bushes of a park. He was all wet, cold and shivering, so I put him in my coat and carried him home. Mother commented on me being just like my Dad and was not happy with the prospect of another dog. I understood her concern because even though my brothers were gone it was still myself and my two younger sisters sharing a one-bedroom house with my parents. There was never enough room for the family let alone another dog.

I called the new puppy Pudgy because he was just a little rolly, polly ball of fun. Butchie took a liking to him and as they played Pudgy would follow the big dog everywhere.

One day Butchie began to chase a car and Pudgy followed. But because he was smaller and slower he didn't get out of the way fast enough and the car hit him. I ran out of the house screaming at the woman driver. "You killed him! You killed him!" I shrieked over and over. Inconsolable, I picked Pudgy up and cradled him in my arms until he was gone.

I was furious. Nothing the woman could say would ease my pain. My face shot daggers at her.

After that, my relationship with Butchie changed. I still loved him but we played less. I blamed him for Pudgy's death too. That little bundle of joy was gone. That little rolly, polly puppy was now buried in our side yard.

A test came shortly afterwards. Butchie had another secret bad habit. If he was out of the house when I left for school, he would follow me, without me knowing. One day at recess there was a lot of noise coming from the area between the senior high building and ours. One of my friends called out to me, "The dog catcher has your dog."

I ran outside and saw Butchie tethered with a group of dogs that had been captured. While the dog catcher was distracted, I ran into the group of dogs and let Butchie loose. Now that I think of it, I should have let them all loose.

Unfortunately, the next time the dog catcher got him we were too late.

Learning to Care for Injuries

One midnight as Father walked home from the afternoon shift he found a puppy whose right side and front right leg were injured. The next day we took him to the vet who told us someone had poured boiling water on the young dog. He warned us that he did not think the puppy would survive, but he would keep him at the clinic overnight. The vet said that if the puppy survived the night he had a chance for a full life.

The next day we got the call from the vet that the puppy had lived and would require extensive care. The vet knew my family would not be able to pay for him to be cared for at the clinic. So, he suggested that if we were willing to follow his strict instructions, we could come and get him.

As the vet showed Father and I exactly what had to be done he explained that the puppies right eye had been burned also. It would fall on my shoulders to do most of the caring. He was to be fed only cooked oatmeal for a week or two. Three times a day I would have to rub his bare skin where the fur had been burned off on his right side and leg with glycerin to make sure it did not dry and crack. I would have to apply a salve to the fur area around the wound and pull off any dead fur so that it did not get gangrenous. Then three times a day I would have to force a huge horse pill down the puppy's throat. The pills were antibiotics required to stave off any infection.

I was too young to realize what I had undertaken, and I was determined to help the puppy get well. We named him Midnight in honor of the time Dad found him and because his fur was completely black.

Each day as I treated Midnight he would wince in pain. But he never bit me or tried to escape. He had surrendered to the care, and I soon recognized that he could not see me if I approached him from the right side.

Mother would not allow any animal to stay upstairs in the house at night. So I made him a bed on the concrete basement floor hoping he would be warm and dry.

The daily care worked well and he began to pick himself up and hobble about after a week, no more cleaning of soiled bedding. Within a few weeks he could have dog food, the first time we bought canned. I knew he would be fine when one day after school Mother greeted me with, "You better do something about that dog, he is ruining the toilet paper."

I opened the trap door to the basement and saw an entire roll of toilet paper strewn across every part of the floor, wrapped around the coal furnace, intertwined around the wash tub. Midnight was fine.

I began taking him outside for walks and he was the first dog attached to the clothes line to roam the yard.

One day he got loose, and no amount of calling out his name would get him to come to me. Then I got the bright idea to get the leash I walked him with. I swung the leash in front of me and called out, "Midnight, do you want to go for a walk?"

To my surprise he ran towards me and allowed me to hook the leash to his collar. Of course I took him for a walk before bringing him back into the house.

Midnight was a sweet and shy dog except if you came up on his right side from behind. Then he would growl.

By the time I left for college my youngest sister had become his second best buddy next to Father.

Midnight lived the longest of our dogs, eleven years, even though he was lost at one point for a week.

One night, without Dad knowing, Midnight had followed his car quite a few miles. When he lost sight or the scent he stopped to wait for Dad's return at a railroad crossing in the next town. Midnight did not return that evening.

Fortunately, Dad took the same route the next week and saw Midnight sitting on the side of the road. Thirsty and hungry, Dad had to lift him into the car. He recovered.

All passing of our pets are painful but Midnight's more than perhaps most. He went missing again, this time for ten days. Then my Father found his body in some bushes on a road a few blocks below our house. Dad was so devastated that he took Midnight's body to the back of the local cemetery and buried him. He would not tell my youngest sister where the body was buried even though she, at 15 years old, was devastated as well. Midnight was her best friend, and probably Dad's as well.

PART THREE – My Work with the Care, Death and Rebirth of Pets

It All Began with a Rescued Thoroughbred Horse

I had been working with Esoteric (Energy) Healing for a few years and had a budding business built on referrals.

One day a woman called and introduced herself by explaining how she heard of me and my work. During a flight to Seattle for Thanksgiving she was sitting in the coach section when a stewardess offered her an upgrade to first class. Sitting down in her new seat she exchanged greetings with the businessman next to her. After a few minutes of pleasant conversation, the gentleman asked if she had heard about me and the work I do. He then went on to explain how I had helped him with some family and business issues and how pleased he was with the results. She asked for my contact information and he handed her one of my business cards.

I believe that I am always in the right place at the right time. And, I know that the individuals I am able to assist are drawn to me, but this story was stretching me to new heights of understanding. I did not make this chance meeting between one of my clients and this new person, M.K. happen. All of the efforts that I could put forth would never have been able to figure out all the logistics to create the connection. Yet, here she was on the phone telling me of her experience and asking me for help.

After working with her for several sessions on some business and relationship issues, she phoned in a panic and asked if I ever worked with animals. I explained that I could but had never made it a big part of my business. She told me her horse was injured and would not let her get close to him. I preferred that she not give me any details of the accident or injuries as I wanted to see if I could sense these with my skills as an Esoteric Healing Facilitator. I told her I would work with her horse remotely; in other words, I did not have to go to the stable in person to do the energy work. I was well trained in remote viewing. She agreed.

Because the accident had just happened and the horse was in need of assistance, I cleared my calendar and decided to work on him immediately. I tuned into him and could feel that his rear flanks were injured on both sides. As I worked with him balancing the different organs and areas of his form there was a pronounced shift in his energy. When I finished, a deep and overwhelming energy of love and gratitude came upon me and I fell to my knees. I was overcome with humility at the energy I could feel. I knew beyond a doubt Slew City knew who I was and what I had done on his behalf and that he was showing me his thankfulness energetically. The horse was blessing me with appreciation. Wow!

When I called M. K. to tell her what I found, she confirmed my findings of the injuries. She then explained that he was terrified of trailers and when she tried to get him into one to take him to the vet, he ran forward and tried to get out the people door, which is not big enough for a horse. She said she would go down to the barn to check on him and call me back. Thirty minutes later she phoned and said that his demeanor had changed and he let her touch him. The fear in his eyes was gone and he was relaxed.

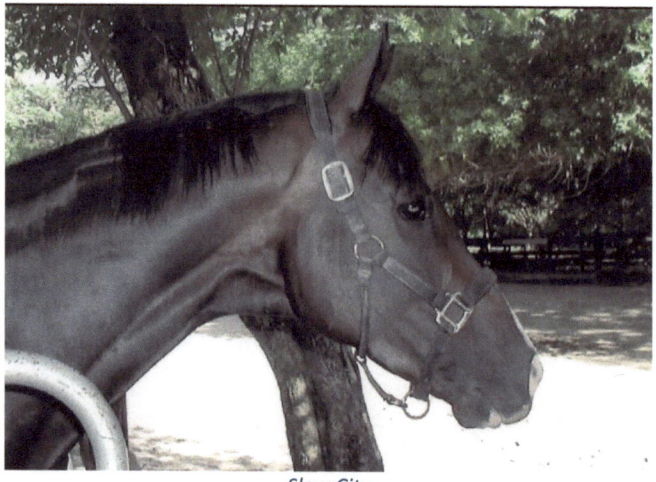

Slew City

Since then my work has included an assortment of dogs and cats with their owners. Some had ailments and injuries, some needed their energy balanced because of emotional issues, others were ready to make their transition, while a few wanted to come back to their friends. Here are just a few examples.

One Dog Ready to Make Her Transition

Thovi was a Husky who had been a longtime companion of a dear friend, Anne and her family. I first met Thovi when I was visiting Anne in Manhattan. She greeted me at the door with a low rumbling "Ohhh" groan of welcome before her housemate, a tiny cat, Macy could take over.

I was in Manhattan to present a workshop on Radical Forgiveness for a group of Anne's friends.

During my stay I asked Anne if I could assist in any way and she requested that I check her dog energetically since she seemed lethargic. I found some energy deficiencies in her adrenals and bladder and showed Anne a few simple things to do to keep the energy balanced.

Several months after my return to Milwaukee, Anne called with more concerns about her beloved dog.

When I tuned into Thovi, the problem in her bladder, kidneys and adrenals had become more acute. Again, I balanced the energies. Anne said she would be taking her to the vet just to make sure. A few days later she called with sad news. Thovi had advanced liver and kidney cancer. She asked again if I could work on her. When I did, I heard inwardly, "I'll be gone by Tuesday."

This was Thursday and I knew the news would be devastating for Anne, but I had no choice. After telling her what I found and heard she commented that the vet did not think it was that advanced.
I was quiet. I have learned that when an animal is ready to go, it is better to accept the idea with grace.

Anne said, "We will see."

Then she called me on Saturday to say that Thovi was in high spirits and going for walks in Riverside Park near her home. She was sure I was wrong.

I checked Thovi's energy and found the same problems, but said nothing.

Tuesday came and I was caught up in work when the phone rang, it was Anne. Because of her deep love and affection, she had spent much of the weekend on the floor with Thovi asking her to let her know if she wanted to go.

She had taken Thovi for a walk that morning and she seemed fine. But when they got back to their building she would not go in. She looked at her favorite fountain for splashing and wouldn't go there either.

Thovi

It was a sunny day and Thovi normally hated being in the sun on a hot day. But, Anne said, "She just laid down and would not move." That evening, with a heavy heart, Anne took her to the vet's and had her quietly put down.

A few months later, Anne's life changed in many ways. First she left for a lengthy teaching trip to Japan, then she moved out of state. It was obvious to me that Thovi knew she was too sick to handle all the changes. Such is the way of our animals. They are much more aware and more surrendered than we can ever imagine.

Puppies from a Dying Mother

Two of my clients are part of rescue organizations. L.R. was called about a sad situation where a breeder had let a Golden Retriever mother die in the hot sun amidst her litter of puppies. Once seeing the group, she decided to take two, a brother and sister and named them Rocky and Jessie. After having them a short time she called me to check on Rocky, he was lethargic and had been diagnosed with kidney problems. When we looked up kidney issues in Louise Hays' book, *Heal Your Body*, it indicated the mental cause could be shame, disappointment, or failure.

When I energetically tuned in to Rocky, I felt this great grief, which was understandable, having witnessed the death of his mother. But then I felt a weight of responsibility and found that Rocky was sad because he could not save his mother or make her well. We also learned he didn't think he deserved to play and have fun.
What an eye opener. So many individuals think that animals have no feelings or do not comprehend loss.

But here was proof positive, this young male pup was disappointed because he could not protect his mother.

After working with him and balancing his energy centers, L.R. reported that he was much more playful and happy.

Animals have so much to teach and share with us.

Rocky Playing

Finding the Right Dog to Rescue

Laura and her husband, Dave, rescue senior Labrador Retrievers. When they first approached me about working with their dog, Bauer, it was to help Bauer stop growling at Dave. With Esoteric Healing there was some improvement. However, when Bauer passed and they were looking for a new dog to rescue I suggested they allow me to check the animal's energy field to assure a match with the family before the next adoption.

Laura called me when they found a few dogs to choose from and we checked each candidate. By balancing each dog with the family we were able to find the right match, a beautiful black Lab who had been rescued as a

Bo

stray and named Moose. They renamed him Bo and this time they have a dog that gets along with everyone in the family.

Because they rescue older Labs the relationship often lasts only a few years. So when Bo passed it was again an opportunity to find another dog.

On this occasion something very interesting happened. Normally, their daughter, E does not fit into the equation for finding the next dog. She is friendly with the dogs but isn't as interested or involved as her parents. However, when Laura gave me the first dog to test, I was intuitively guided to check for energetic harmony with E. There was none and I heard inwardly, "This dog will not like the child."

I was taken aback and called Laura to explain my findings. She was also surprised as the paperwork said that the dog lived with children. We will never know why but we moved on and found the perfect match in Zac.

Zac

Finding Your Pet After Death

A few people who have heard about my dog coming back to me have asked me to help them with beloved cats and dogs ready to make their transition.

Barb, our pet sitter, is one such person. Her cat Kiki was nearing the end of his life. I told her to remind him during his last days that she would love to have him back. Once he passed we talked about the timing required before his return.

Nonetheless she began her search way too early. And, several times she asked me to check to see if he was back in the body, which one can energetically detect. He was not.

Finally, after waiting for enough time to pass, she called about some Himalayan kittens she found in Spooner, WI which is quite a distance away. I suggested she ask for photos first. When she received the pictures of the three kittens she called me to check the energy.
I asked her to hold one picture at a time to her heart without telling me what her feeling was. When I checked the energy between she and the first it was so powerful I was surprised.

I then asked her to hold each of the other photos to her heart one at a time just to make sure. The next kitten had harmonious energy but not as powerful. However, the third kitten had none. Then Barb said: "The energy with the first kitten was so powerful, I began to cry. I believe the second kitten is also a former cat of mine. I am going to purchase both of them because I believe they were together before as Caesar and Marcus. Now their names are Zeus and Apollo

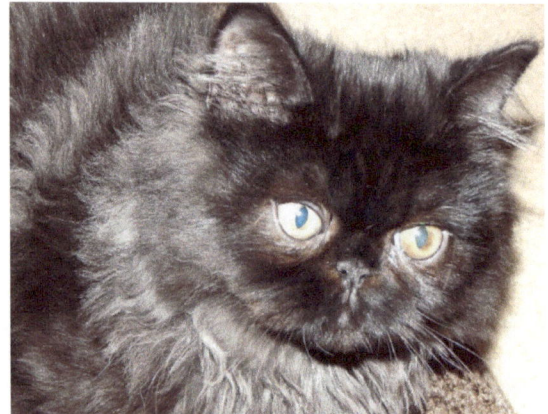

Zeus

Apollo

Barb's final remarks about the event: "It was the most profound experience I have had with you to have Kiki come back. It was actually overwhelming when I felt his energy. My heart burst open and I began to cry. You really helped me to find him and the right mate for him.

To me this has been a very good experience because you made me realize that it is possible to reconnect with our pets after they have passed on and been reborn."

An Alaskan Spitz Returns As ....

Barb's Alaskan Spitz, Jules, had also been ailing but she didn't want to do anything about him until she had resolved her situation with Kiki.

Being elderly, Jules had a hard time walking. I cautioned Barb to remind him that she would like him to come back in case he left abruptly. She could see that he was overcome by the new kittens and that he was no fun for them either.

After a great deal of struggle and praying for guidance she decided it would be best to put him down on his birthday, November 11th. As always, it was a very difficult decision, yet she knew that Jules needed to be freed from his pain and discomfort.

She reminded him several times of her love and her desire for him to return. Her husband, Bob, also comforted him with the thought of returning to their home.

After he passed, her experience with the kittens and the timing made it a bit easier for her to relax and wait. However, she was having a hard time finding a breeder of Alaskan Spitz's, the only breed she ever owned, who would be having litters in the time we had calculated.

Jules

I reminded her of how my dog came back to me. Being our dog sitter she was very familiar with the story as she had witnessed Chakotay's decline and then our reunion.

One day when she was at my office for an Esoteric treatment of her own, I offered to look online with her to see if we could find Jules. I got an intuitive hit that he might come back through Chakotay's breeder. So we went to the site and began to look at new puppies.

Both of us were enamored with a little two-tone brown puppy with amazing eyes. Barb said, "I think that's Jules." I agreed.

I checked his energy and got a resounding, "Yes."

Barb called up the breeder to reserve the puppy and it was hers. His name is Cosmo.

Cosmo

I believe we must acknowledge our rightful place as caretakers of the portion of the planet we inhabit. We have a sacred pact with the animals that pass through our lives as well as the greater life all around. Therefore, we cannot ignore or deny the important place our pets play as they teach, comfort, correct and love us. They are and always will be an immensely important part of our lives.

Karen A. Bowen's work with animals is part of a larger service where she assists individuals with a variety of needs and backgrounds. Parents, children, couples, entrepreneurs, as well as, PhD's, and professionals all benefit from her ability to identify the limiting beliefs and obstacles preventing their success. Using the modalities of Energy Psychology, Radical Forgiveness and Esoteric Healing, Karen helps each individual remove the blocks, gain new insight, and reclaim their power to create the life they love.

Many know Karen as a wise and trusted mentor and friend.

She says, "I am present to remind each person of their power of creation and to assist them in removing whatever obstacles block their path to fulfilling their heart's desire."

Karen is also the originator of the Authentic Triangle. She teaches numerous workshops, is a published author, and nationally known public speaker, whose special skill is to teach how life works and how to make spiritual laws practical in our everyday lives.

She lives in the Midwest with her pets and her husband Richard A. Bowen who is also an author.

For Information or an appointment,
Website: www.karenabowen.com
Email: karenabowen@att.net

www.ingramcontent.com/pod-product-compliance
Lightning Source LLC
Chambersburg PA
CBHW042217050426
42453CB00001BA/2